Cha

The  and the  ran.

The  ran past the .

He ran past the cat.

He ran past the sand.

The  ran and ran.

The  sat.

"I can nap," he said.

Chapter 2

See the  .

He can pass the cat and the sand.

He can pass the  .

The  pants and pants.

He is at the camp!

The  sees the  .

What a sad  !

What a happy  !